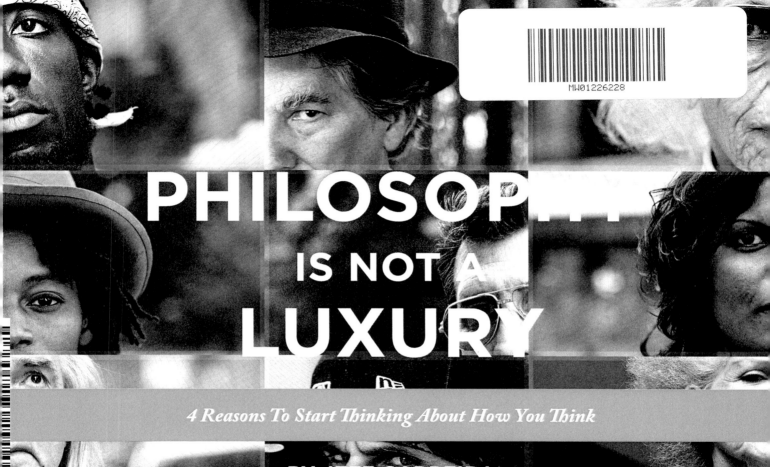

PHILOSOPHY IS NOT A LUXURY

4 Reasons To Start Thinking About How You Think

BY JEFF CARREIRA

PHOTOGRAPHS BY SIMON HØGSBERG

Philosophy Is Not A Luxury
Four Reasons To Start Thinking About How You Think
by Jeff Carreira

Copyright © 2013 Emergence Education

Emergence Education
PO Box 429
Lenox, MA 01240

ISBN-13: 9780615808802
ISBN-10: 0615808808

Book Design by www.choosefreeagency.com
Photographs by Simon Högsberg

contents

Introduction 3

Reason one:
The world is not the way you think it is 6

    1. The Myth of the Given 8

    2. The Creation of Reality 12

    3. Radical Inquiry 15

Reason two:
You may not be who you think you are 19

    4. The Stream of Consciousness 21

    5. Process and Free Will 23

    6. A Habit of Identification 26

Reason three:
We don't know, and yet we have to act as if we do 31

    7. Fallibilism 33

    8. The Reality of the Unknown 37

    9. Evolutionary Existentialism 40

Reason four:
The circumstances around us are changing faster than we can 44

    10. Our Evolutionary Crisis 46

    11. Philosophy is Not a Luxury 49

This book is about the profound utility of philosophy. It is rooted in the conviction that philosophy is not a luxury—it is a necessity that none of us can afford to ignore.

This book is not an instruction manual for inquiry or a collection of philosophical ideas to adopt. I have not written it in order to tell you what to think, but rather to give you some things to think about. In doing this I am following a Romantic sentiment that recognizes that the true value of writing lies beyond the understanding contained in the words. It is the truth provoked by the words in the heart and mind of the reader that is the ultimate measure of a writing's success. Ralph Waldo Emerson, one of the first American men of letters, insisted that truth and real understanding must be birthed within us and not merely passed along secondhand:

> Truly speaking, it is not instruction, but provocation, that I can receive from another soul.

I have organized this book around four provocative statements:

1. The world is not the way you think it is.

2. You may not be who you think you are.

3. We don't know, and yet we have to act as if we do.

4. The circumstances around us are changing faster than we can.

Don't just read this book—think about it.

Each of these statements is presented as a good reason to start thinking about how you think. I have separated the book into four sections, each beginning with one of the above statements. The statement is followed by a few sentences that create a framework for contemplation about it, two or three short essays, and a few concluding sentences.

Don't just read this book—think about it.

My advice is to read vulnerably, not critically. Give less of your attention to the words on the page and more to where the words can take you. Follow your own understanding, not mine. To quote Emerson again:

> The foregoing generations beheld God and nature face

to face; we, through their eyes. Why should not we also enjoy an original relation to the universe?

My first intention in writing this book is, as I have already stated, to give you some things to think about and to create a context for thinking about how you think. My second objective is to educate you (especially if you happen to be an American) about some of the ideas that are part of the rich tradition of American philosophy.

The American character is diverse and somewhat contradictory, but one trait generally associated with it is pragmatism. Americans like things that work. That might be why the "love of philosophy" is not one of the characteristics most often associated with Americans. And it is probably not surprising that the greatest American philosophers have all insisted that philosophy is only worthwhile if it serves as a tool for living better lives and facing life's challenges.

The philosophical ideas most discussed in this book are those held by the classical American philosophers Charles Sanders Peirce, William James, and John Dewey. These three brilliant minds were the originators of the philosophy called pragmatism, which remains to this day America's most significant contribution to world philosophy.

The essays included here represent a general progression of thought, each building upon the last. I suggest, however, you read them as complete in themselves and see what questions and avenues for further inquiry they open up for you. Each essay is a snapshot, a glimpse into an extraordinary perspective on reality. They are seeds for contemplation, starting points for your own inquiry.

reason

ONE

THE WORLD IS NOT THE WAY YOU THINK IT IS.

We look out at the world, and we assume that it is the way
it appears to be.
It's not.
The world may be the way it is, but our perception of it is
seldom completely accurate & probably never will be.
Knowing this is really important.

The following short essays illustrate how some great minds have tackled the problem of perception and the way the world actually is.

THE MYTH
OF THE GIVEN

Our lives are governed by ideas. The way you see and respond to the world is a product of the ideas you believe in. The great American psychologist and philosopher William James realized this and taught that the most important capacity that human beings have is "the will to believe." James didn't think that we could choose our actions because they are dictated to us by the ideas we believe in. What we can do is consciously choose which ideas we believe in. From there the beliefs will unfold into action of their own accord, but at least we have exercised our will to believe.

This book asks you to examine your beliefs. To discover what you actually know firsthand and what you have learned secondhand and take on faith. Most of us take more on faith than we realize. We all know, for instance, that the Earth revolves around the Sun. We learned that in elementary school. But do we actually have any direct evidence of it? If we look up at the sky, what we see is the Sun going around the Earth. We have been told that it is the other way around. We accept the truth of it and assume that someone has or has had direct evidence of it. We all believe many things that we accept on faith and assume that we have good reason to do so.

During the mid-twentieth century, the American philosopher Wilfrid Sellars opened a line of inquiry into the assumptions behind what we think we know. He gave a famous series of lectures about what he called "the myth of the given." The simplest way to understand what he was getting at is to say that the world is not always the way it appears to be. The world doesn't just exist; it appears to us—and the way it appears is not necessarily the way it is. The world presents itself to us through layers of interpretation. William James talked about our experience of the world as being "thick"—thick with layers of meaning and significance that are ultimately interpretations of reality, not reality in an objective sense.

Most of us probably don't have a problem with this—after all, we all know that we don't always see things clearly. And yet if we ask deeper questions about life and existence we may come upon a point where we don't want to ask any more questions. At that point we can fall into two traps. One is the way of the fundamentalist, who holds tenaciously to what he or she already believes to be true in spite of evidence to the contrary. The other is the way of the cynic, who concludes that there is ultimately no way to know what is true. In both cases we give ourselves an excuse not to question any further.

This book is offering a different possibility—the way of perpetual inquiry. On this path we don't see truth as an end point to settle into, but as a jumping-off point to further inquiry. Each truth is a temporary stepping stone that offers just enough stability to launch off of into the next inquiry and the next discovery of truth. On this path our questioning is not converging toward a final answer. It is opening up into the discovery of new questions and new truths.

If we seriously consider the possibility of embarking wholeheartedly on a path of perpetual inquiry, we may find even more resistance arising. After all, you can't question everything. There has to be something real and solid and true somewhere. There is no way for us to follow every perception or idea back to some point of origin that will validate it. Of course this is true. We can't follow every thought back to its source. Because it is my position that we must find a way to remain open to the profound uncertainty inherent in what we perceive to be real.

The world doesn't just exist; it appears to us— and the way it appears is not necessarily the way it is.

Another way to think about the myth of the given is as the deeply held belief that underneath the appearance of reality there is something that we can safely assume is actually real and true—something that is just given.

Most of us first encountered the idea of "the given" in our high school physics classes. Remember? You start a physics problem with a list of givens. For instance, if you know the distance a car travels and the time it took to go that distance, you can calculate the average speed of the car. The basic idea is that as long as you know a sufficient number of facts you can use the rules of logic to derive new facts. These new facts will be true because they are based on previously known "givens."

In our everyday thinking we don't always realize what we are assuming to be "given." What we accept as real is built on a mountain of assumptions the size and scale of which we are unaware of. The ideas and concepts that we know of are the tip of the iceberg, like an island of thought that is actually the tip of a mountain of assumptions that are hidden in the murky depths of the unconscious. These assumptions have built up over our own lifetime and throughout the history of the human mind.

As human understanding has been built up through centuries of thought, the ideas of one generation become the unconscious assumptions of the next. On and on, generation after generation, age to age, this process continues leading right up to the ideas in our own minds. When we begin to realize how many assump-tions lie behind our thinking, we start to wonder, as I believe Sellars did, if there is anything truly un-derived and rock-solid true underneath it all. Maybe we are sitting on a mountain of assumptions built on other assumptions built on other assumptions, all the way to the bottom.

What we assume to be reality as we look out at the world is not necessarily objectively real at all. It is a perspective on reality that is constructed through a lens of ideas and attitudes that have been personally developed and culturally inherited and that we are largely not even aware of. One trend in philosophy known as deconstructionism can be understood as the attempt to uncover the "real" truth by stripping our assumptions away and seeing what is left. Whatever is left is really real.

But this seems to imply that in order to find reality we have to strip ourselves out of the picture. And that makes us, in some fundamental way, the unreal part of the universe.

There might be a better way to look at it. What would happen if we didn't define reality as what exists when we are not there, but instead assert that reality includes whatever was there before us as well as our perception of it?

This would mean that reality is not something separate from us that we perceive. It is a process of growth that includes the growth of our perception of it. Our perception of reality does not exist in isolation from reality; it is part of reality. Reality is not a static thing out there that is passively observed—it is a growing thing that evolves as we do.

This evolutionary view of reality as a holistic process of growth that includes us is central to the American philosophy called pragmatism, and I will explore different aspects of that philosophy in the remaining essays of this book.

two

THE CREATION OF REALITY

As I mentioned briefly at the close of the last essay, the American philosophy of pragmatism is of particular interest to me. Pragmatism is the most significant genuinely American contribution to world philosophy. Charles Sanders Peirce and William James are generally considered to be the original founders of pragmatism, with John Dewey joining them early on and becoming the leading proponent of this way of thinking until the middle of the twentieth century.

To place the first American pragmatists in historical context, we must recognize that they were following in the footsteps of the great German idealist Immanuel Kant. In 1781 Kant published *The Critique of Pure Reason* and forever changed the world of philosophy. What Kant articulated was that reality as we perceive it is not purely pre-existent and objective; it is also, at least partly, constructed and subjective.

It is easy to believe that reality as we see it is a reflection of reality as it actually is. In other words, we tend to assume that the function that the mind plays is passive, like a mirror that doesn't alter the image of reality that it reflects to us. But doesn't this view of reality leave us disconnected from the world?

When we talk about objective reality, what we commonly mean is that which is real even if we are not around. Objective reality—the real world—has a reality independent of us. That means that if something is objectively real I will see it the same way that everyone else does. If two or more people see things differently, they can't all be seeing what is objectively real. To get to what is true we would have to strip away any errors in perception or biases that any one of us might be holding.

We tend to assume that the function that the mind plays is passive, like a mirror ...

And that is the way we tend to think about reality. Reality, we imagine, is what is left when we are not adding anything to the picture. It already exists, and we just need to see it clearly. To get from our interpreted picture of reality to an accurate picture of reality all we need to do is strip away all of the interpretation, and then we move closer and closer to the real world. In a sense we are stripping ourselves out of the picture to find reality. But that

seems to place us outside of reality. Is reality something that exists independently of us? Are we outside of reality looking in at it?

Not so, said Kant. The universe is not a static thing that is simply discovered. It is an organic, growing thing that is created—in part by us. Our perception may originate with sensations of an objective reality that is independent of us, but those perceptions are ordered, organized, categorized, and arranged into reality as we perceive it. Kant was articulating a possibility for how we might have an active and creative role in the unfolding of reality.

According to Kant, there is a part of reality—the noumenon—that we can't know directly, and another part of reality—the phenomenon—that we do perceive. Reality includes both, and our perception of reality is directly influenced and in some ways constructed by our own minds. Out of a myriad of physical, emotional, and conceptual sensations that enter into our awareness, we are only aware of a small part, and those are compiled into reality as we see it.

One of Kant's profound insights is that the picture of reality that we construct has to remain consistent through time with our previous conceptions of reality. All of the incoming information that we receive has to be arranged to create a picture that does not conflict with the past. In this way we create a unity between the present moment and all past moments. If we did not, our experience of reality would break apart into an unintelligible chaos of random occurrences.

Kant understood human reason to be a constantly integrative process. We are bombarded with varied and largely incoherent sensations. These sensations are then filtered, ordered, and congealed into a coherent picture of reality. This consistent picture of reality Kant referred to as "necessary transcendental unity," and he saw it as the contextual background of all of our experience. The demand that this contextual background remain coherent from moment to moment places a constant demand on the way we order our perceptions.

Kant placed human beings squarely inside of the creative process of reality. This profound connection between human perception and the creation of reality set the stage for all of Western philosophy to follow. And the American pragmatists were building on Kant's insight with the added twist that they connected reality not only to human perception, but to human activity as well. In their view, reality is in a significant way actually created by our actions. According to pragmatism—at least in the William James version—ideas are not true in themselves; they become true when acted upon and proven valid. Reality is created as we live it out.

three

RADICAL
INQUIRY

Of all the American pragmatists Charles Sanders Peirce was following most directly along the lines of thought that had been explored by Kant. Kant, in his attempt to save the world from skepticism, insisted that there did have to be some givens—some things that we can count on—and he imagined twelve categories of such a priori or "before everything else" truths, including the laws of time, space, and causality. Peirce, like Kant, also believed that the universe had to have started with something, and one of his early attempts to identify what that something was can be found in a short paper he wrote called "Design and Chance." He read his paper on January 17, 1884, to the members of the Metaphysical Club, which he founded at Johns Hopkins University. In it Peirce asks fundamental philosophical questions such as, Do real things exist? and Does causality have a cause? with a wild openness that appears to be dramatically free of predispositions and preferred outcomes. His unbridled willingness to follow logic

---

down whatever path it led him was surely the source of his creative genius.

One of the speculations Peirce offers is his certainty that someday the measurement of the angles of a triangle formed between two distant stars and the Earth would prove to us that space was, in fact, curved. Peirce insisted that the only reason we had not yet been able to confirm the curvature of space by measuring the angles of triangles was simply because we had not yet managed to measure a triangle big enough.

Peirce goes on to question the fundamental categories of reality and in particular some of those imagined by Immanuel Kant. And he did so in light of the new understanding of evolution that Darwin's recent publication of *On the Origin of Species* had brought to the world. The Kantian categories included space, time, and causality, and together, so Kant proposed, they create the framework for what we experience as reality. Most of us assume that the universe evolved within a container of time, space, and causality, much like a calf grows to be a cow within the container of a farm. Peirce took exception to this notion. If time, space, and causality are part of the universe, they must also have evolved. This deceptively simple notion may seem obvious at first glance, but its implications are enormous.

Why are moments in time ordered sequentially? Maybe the first moments appeared in random order—one appears now in the year 2012; the next ten days in the past; then one four months in the future; then one a thousand years in the past; and on and on. Perhaps those moments that happened by chance to appear in sequential order had a "survival advantage," and soon all of the nonsequential moments died out of existence. Maybe that is why we only find sequential moments in the universe today. And finding the universe as it is we imagine that that is how it must always have been. The same may be true with space; perhaps adjacent spots in space were not always adjacent. And again with causality, maybe things happened randomly initially, and causality only gradually developed. Peirce's radical inquiry gives us a glimpse of how much we take for granted as "real" that, when considered more deeply, turn out to be unquestioned and unproven assumptions.

And finding the universe as it is we imagine that that is how it must always have been.

What we are confronted with in Peirce could be thought of as evolutionary skepticism. Because he recognized how miniscule we are in the infinite expanse of cosmic evolution, Peirce assumed that everything we thought to be true was only relatively true—in the sense that it is true for entities of about our size, with physiological and psychological characteristics like ours, living on a planet similar to our Earth, at about this time in its history within the context of the much larger history of the universe of which it is a tiny part.

Peirce was driven to determine what the essential characteristics of our evolving universe were. What features must have existed at the birth of the universe in order for evolution to be possible? In his inquiry Peirce identifies two absolutely necessary characteristics.

The first of these characteristics is the ability for spontaneous creation—happenings that occur by pure chance. In order for evolution to occur, Peirce realized, there must be at a bare minimum the possibility for something new to appear from nowhere and out of nothing. If this were not the case, nothing could possibly have ever arisen that could ultimately have led to the universe. But the possibility of novelty alone is not enough because any universe that contained only the ability for novelty would be doomed to total chaos. New and unrelated events would continually explode into existence in a never ending cascade of confusion. So Peirce claimed that evolution requires a second characteristic—the ability to form habits. This is the tendency for something that has already happened once to be more likely to happen again. This tendency toward habit assures that some degree of order will form in our universe.

So an evolving universe only requires two elements as a starting point: the ability to change and the tendency to stick. The universe is change that sticks. The image of evolution that Peirce evokes is one of pure possibility out of which something—and, being spontaneous, there's no telling what—bursts into being. Soon other "somethings" burst into being, and each becomes more likely to happen again once it occurs. Thus the universe begins its evolutionary flow, one that consists of events that happen and tend to happen again and again. Slowly, from nothing but possibility, the universe grows.

Mind, matter, life, nonlife is all one flowing mass of being that, at its very bottom, has only two characteristics—spontaneous chance and the tendency to form habits. Reality is a surge of existence that pours out like liquid through time. And that liquid is not equally fluid everywhere. In some places it is thin and runs like water, passing quickly from one form to another. In other places it is viscous like oil or gelatin and oozes slowly from shape to shape, remaining fixed for a time before reforming. In still others the liquid runs more like glass, flowing so slowly that its movement can only be seen across vast expanses of time.

ARE WE OUTSIDE OF REALITY LOOKING IN?

Is our experience of reality simply a perceptual illusion?

Are we outside of reality looking in?

Or is our perception of reality also part of reality?

Is the world a collection of objects that we look at from the outside?

Or is the world a flowing river of change and habit with nothing solid to it?

reason
TWO

YOU MAY NOT BE WHO YOU THINK YOU ARE.

We think we are a "something"—an entity that
emerged in the universe on a planet called Earth.
Are we really?
What is a human being? What am I?
Am I my body, my brain, my thoughts?
Superficially, it seems that we are simply some
combination of all of these things and more.
When you look deeply, the simple question,
Who am I? reveals mindboggling complexity.

The following essays outline some of the ways that the American pragmatist philosophers thought about who we are.

four

THE STREAM OF CONSCIOUSNESS

To understand the thinking of William James I have tried to see the world as I believe he saw it—as one continuous, unfolding flow. In my own contemplation of James I have followed a line of thought that mirrors in some ways his own development from a psychologist to a philosopher. James' philosophic pet peeve was any notion of duality, which means any belief in the existence of any realm of being outside of, or separate from, the rest of reality. James believed that the universe had to be one continuous, unbroken event, and he was at war with metaphysical or transcendental dualisms that allowed for two separate parts of reality to exist simultaneously.

In his early psychological writing James vividly described how our experience of consciousness emerges as a continuous, single stream. His conception of "the stream of consciousness" holds tremendous implications about our experience of self-consciousness and the ultimate nature of who we are.

Our experience appears to be that while we are aware of an object we are also aware of being aware of the object—we are self-consciously aware of the object. The same thing happens for actions. We are acting, and we are simultaneously aware that we are acting. Most of us assume that there exists both the original awareness of the object AND at the same time a simultaneous awareness of being aware of the object or of the action. Essentially we imagine a split in our consciousness. There is a "me" that is aware of the object AND another "me" that is aware of the "me being aware of the object." So where does that second "me" exist? If you think about it, you will probably realize that you don't usually think about it. If you do think about it, you might picture the awareness of yourself being aware as somehow hovering over the self that sees in the first place. The self that sees is on the ground seeing, and the self that is aware of the self that sees is hovering above. The hovering self is a transcendent self that exists outside of the original seeing or the original action and watches.

There is only an experience of being aware of a sense of self that periodically appears in the stream of consciousness.

Because he insisted that consciousness had to be a continuous stream and that self-awareness couldn't be separate from that stream, James concluded that the awareness of self was simply another experience in the ongoing flow of consciousness. Self-awareness in this way becomes not a separate vantage point from which to view myself viewing the object, but rather my self-awareness is just another experience in the train of experience that is the stream of consciousness. At one moment I am aware only of the object, and then in the next moment I am aware of myself, and then in the next moment I am aware of myself being aware of the object, and in the next moment I am aware of the object again, and so on, one experience after another in a continuous flow. There is no transcendent self; there is only an experience of being aware of a sense of self that periodically appears in the stream of consciousness.

In James' later philosophy he took this idea one step further and stated that the world itself is created from successive moments of experience. Experience is the "stuff" that reality is made of. And reality, like consciousness, appears drop by drop in one continuous stream. He didn't see ideas as existing outside of the world pointing back to it. The physical world of objects and the mental world of thoughts and feelings were both made up of "pure experience."

five

PROCESS AND
FREE WILL

William James, who was trained as a medical doctor at Harvard Medical School, is often said to be America's first great psychologist. His first and arguably most significant written work was *The Principles of Psychology*, published in 1890. James' later philosophical work always retained a certain tendency toward the psychological, and many of his core ideas were initially expressed in this early work.

James is famed to have been the originator of the conception of consciousness as a stream—a continuous succession of experiences. The stream of consciousness is an unending parade of thoughts, feelings, images, ideas, sensations, conceptions, emotions, and so on. Each element of experience passes before our conscious awareness and then passes away. As we discussed earlier, this view leads to a strikingly original conception of how the sense of self is formed. This view of consciousness was not without its problems, and James' lifelong project was to create a clear and comprehensive description of the process through which reality as we experience it unfolds.

One of the issues that arises from the view that consciousness appears in successive chunks is explaining how we come to experience a sense of continuity between past and present moments. James recognized that the lines between the seemingly separate objects of consciousness could not be as hard-edged as we might assume. If each of our experiences were truly completely separate from the one that came before, we would live in a chaos of random experiences that would appear with no connection to the past. One solution to this problem would be the existence of a transcendent self—the second "me" that hovers above the flowing process of experience and is able to see how it is all connected in one continuous stream. James was committed to explaining our experience of reality without having to assume any such transcendent entity.

James realized that there was another way to imagine how the experience of continuity could be explained. It is clear that instead of chaos, our experience is a continuous stream of consciousness in which each moment of experience is immediately recognized to be part of a continuum. James realized that this must mean that the cognitive experiences of each moment must overlap so that each has a "fringe" in front and behind that crosses over into the adjacent moments.

In this way, our present experience includes a tail end of the experience of the preceding moment as it trails off and a leading edge of our next experience as it creeps into awareness.

So James was able to explain our experience of continuity, but there was a second problem with his process view—one that was very personal to James. By describing reality as a single continuous stream of experience, James did away with the need to assume the existence of any observer or active agent. What then did this mean about human free will? As a result of his own conclusions, James was forced to admit in the last chapter of *The Principles of Psychology* that as a science, psychology must assume that human experience is deterministic. In other words, human consciousness and activity flows spontaneously without there being any entity that is making decisions.

James was a strong libertarian and would not personally accept the determinism that even he claimed the evidence seemed to point to. He found the room to insert free will into his ideas by attributing it to the selecting function that the mind played in the process of life. He described the mind as an "organ of selection," choosing what experiences would come into and be held in our conscious awareness. And it was this selecting function that gave human beings the ability to choose their actions.

In an essay entitled "Are we Automata?" James tackled the

question of free will directly. In the essay he concludes that our freedom lies in our ability to choose what we place our attention on. We all seem to have the ability through an act of will to hold our conscious attention on some thoughts to the exclusion of others. Those thoughts held firmly in consciousness will inevitably manifest in action. In this way we perform a selecting function in the stream of experience that effectively makes us the chooser of which thoughts we put our attention on and therefore which thoughts will survive in our conscious awareness long enough to generate action. This is what James called "the will to believe," and it was this ability that allowed human beings to become self-authoring.

What we are most responsible for is the person that we have become, a person based on the choices that we ourselves have freely made.

James considered himself a moral philosopher, and he was a libertarian because he believed that the belief in free will is required as a basis for morality. If the world were deterministic and all of our actions were merely the natural outcome of preexisting circumstances, how can anyone be held responsible for what they do? In his earliest professional writing, James asserts that it is our choices that define us, and ultimately what we are most responsible for is the person that we have become, a person based on the choices that we ourselves have freely made. In his book *Psychology: The Briefer Course*, James explains the ethical context for our choices:

> The ethical energy par excellence has to . . . choose which interest out of several, equally coercive, shall become supreme. The issue here is of the utmost pregnancy, for it decides a man's entire career. When he debates, Shall I commit this crime? choose that profession? accept that office, or marry this fortune?—his choice really lies between one of several equally possible future Characters . . . The problem with the man is less what act he shall now resolve to do than what being he shall now choose to become.

six

A HABIT OF IDENTIFICATION

In the 1870s Charles Sanders Peirce and William James were both members of an informal discussion circle known as the Metaphysical Club. This small group of young Harvard graduates met periodically to discuss ideas of philosophy, religion, and science in light of Charles Darwin's groundbreaking book *On the Origin of Species*, which had been published in 1859. In those meetings the ground for what would become the philosophy of pragmatism was set. John Dewey was not a member of the Metaphysical Club. Dewey was born in 1859 in Burlington, Vermont, and received his original training in philosophy in the Hegelian tradition at the University of Vermont. He was also deeply intrigued by Darwin's ideas, and later when he read James' *The Principles of Psychology* Dewey became a converted pragmatist and would eventually become one of America's most globally influential philosophers.

James had inspired Dewey in part with his bold assertion that there was no transcendent self that acts as the observer of objects and actions. Dewey adopted James' position and took it further by admitting that there was no separate willful entity at the source of our choices and actions in a way that James himself would not accept. According to Dewey, activity happens as a response to the changing environment, not as a consequence of decisions made by a willing agent. Dewey believed that our identification with an illusionary entity called "myself" was itself merely a habit of identification.

Dewey was perplexed with James' strong libertarian belief in free will, especially since James himself had dealt some of the hardest knocks to the notion of "the self" with his own theory of the stream of consciousness. James didn't believe that there was any "self" that existed as the observer of our experience, and yet he had insisted on reserving space for a choosing "self" to exist within the unending stream of experience.

In Dewey's conception of a stream of activity, human action is explained as the unfolding of habits. There is no doer that is guiding action; there are just habitual ways of thinking and acting that have been learned in response to circumstance. As we continually engage with the environment, that encounter stimulates the formation of habits of action, thought, and emotion. As long as there is no disharmony between the environment and our habitual ways of acting, thinking, and feeling, we remain essentially unconscious.

Have you ever gotten up out of bed in the morning, made coffee, taken a shower, got dressed, and left the house without really being aware of it all happening? According to Dewey, the whole process is simply a manifestation of habit. But what happens if just before we leave the house we reach into our coat pocket and realize that we don't have our car keys? At that point we become consciously aware of ourselves and the circumstances around us. There is a disharmony between the environment and our habits that blocks the habit from functioning. Something is out of place, and conscious engagement is required in order to restore the harmonious union of habit and environment.

The impediment of habit awakens us to the urgency and immediacy of life.

The awakening to consciousness that occurs in the face of disharmony, according to Dewey, is an awaking to the impulse of life itself. The impediment of habit awakens us to the urgency and immediacy of life. As Dewey describes it, this awakening is not so much an awakening of a human agent to consciousness, but rather it is an awakening of the life impulse itself through the vehicle of a human form. This life impulse is directed toward the future and compelled to restore the harmony between habit and environment. In human beings this effort to restore harmony initiates a process of conscious thought in which the outcomes of different possible responses are imagined until a course of action promises the satisfactory restoration of harmony and that action is taken. If harmony is restored, we return again to an unconscious relationship to activity. Once we find our keys, we walk out the door and continue on unconsciously until our next encounter with disharmony.

Human freedom in Dewey's philosophy could be increased through the expansion of our ability to think, by which he meant expanding our options for response and our ability to evaluate the relative effectiveness of different possible responses. When confronted with disharmony, the amount of freedom we will be able to exercise in response depends on the depth and breadth of our thought processes because more developed thinking can imagine more possible responses to disharmony.

Of the early American pragmatists Dewey was arguably the most socially oriented, and he thought about social institutions, customs, and norms as habits that develop in society over time. He realized that it is the habits of society that are the active agents, not individuals. We are not acting according to habit; habit is acting itself out through us. As he saw it, human society is a collection of habits that are continuously acting themselves out in human form. As society develops, it is not people that are developing; it is social habits that are developing, and these habits gain expression through the actions of individuals.

Let me illustrate what Dewey was getting at with the example of the common custom of saying hello. Many people are in the habit of saying hello when they meet someone. If you ask them why they do it, they will say that it is the polite thing to do. Essentially they are stating that they are a polite person, and so they say hello because that is what polite people do. But how did the habit of saying hello actually develop in most of us as young children in the first place? Probably our mother, father, or other caretaker repeated the word to us over and over again at different times. One day we successfully imitated what we heard. At that point we had no understanding of what we were saying or even that we were saying anything. We were only imitating the act of making a particular sound. When we managed to imitate the sound clearly enough, someone probably affirmed the act with affection. Through repeated reinforcement of this type, we started to develop the habit of saying hello to everyone we saw.

It was much later, once we had some mastery of language, that we learned that saying hello is polite and that we should be polite. The ideas that there are polite people, that polite people say hello, and that we are a polite person who says hello all developed after the habit of saying hello had already been acquired. We did not start out as a self that then learned to say hello; we started as a habit of saying hello that then learned to identify with an idea of being a self that says hello. What we call a self is really a socially constructed habit of identification.

Dewey became best known for his work in social action and education. His interest in the evolution of culture was fueled by his realization that human society develops through the formation of new cultural habits that manifest as the actions of individuals. Learning this allowed Dewey to see that the future evolution of humanity could be guided and controlled through the conscious formation of new cultural habits, and he dedicated his life to this evolutionary calling.

What we call a self is really a socially constructed habit of identification.

What compelled Dewey most was his recognition that humanity was beginning to uncover the mechanisms through which the entire process of evolution worked. As we began to understand how the universe evolved, we could take responsibility for the future unfolding of that process. A new moral sensibility was being born as human beings became the evolutionary custodians of the future. In an essay entitled "Evolution and Ethics" Dewey describes this new moral awakening:

> The process and the forces bound up with the cosmic have come to consciousness in man. That which was instinct in the animal is conscious impulse in man. That which was "tendency to vary" in the animal is conscious foresight in man. That which was unconscious adaptation and survival in the animal, taking place by the "cut and try" method until it worked itself out, is with man conscious deliberation and experimentation . . . Man in his conscious struggles, in his doubts, temptations, and defeats, in his aspirations and successes, is moved on and buoyed up by the forces which have developed nature; and that in this moral struggle he acts not as a mere individual but as an organ in maintaining and carrying forward the universal process.

WHAT IF YOU DON'T EXIST THE WAY THAT YOU'VE ALWAYS THOUGHT YOU DID?

What if you are not a something that thinks and acts?
What if all of life were one unfolding process that included:
Experiences of thinking
Experiences of acting
And experiences of thinking that you are a something that thinks and acts?

"A man is a method, a progressive arrangement; a selecting principle,
gathering his like to him; wherever he goes."
—Ralph Waldo Emerson

reason

THREE

WE DON'T KNOW AND YET WE HAVE TO ACT AS IF WE DO.

Every step we take, every action, every choice to do anything is ultimately an act of faith.

Most of the time, thankfully, we live with an ongoing sense of certainty.

We imagine that the world is predictable enough to support us.

Then there are those moments in which everything gets swept away. We lose a job, we crash a car, a loved one passes, and we realize that nothing was ever certain.

And yet we have to act as if it is or live paralyzed by doubt.

The following essays show how the American pragmatists taught us to embrace the reality of the unknown.

seven

FALLIBILISM

What are we asserting when we claim that a statement is true? What we most commonly mean is that the words we are using or the idea that we are holding in our mind corresponds to some actual event or thing in the real world. This is known as the correspondence theory of truth. Implicit in this view is that there is some objective world that exists independently of our thoughts and ideas about it. If our ideas are true, then they are accurate representations of the real world. If they are false, then they are misrepresentations of the real world. The mind is seen as playing the part of a mirror that inertly reflects reality. But if this were true, how do we account for errors in thinking and judgment? A mirror never makes a mistake. If you hold a sunflower in front of a mirror, you will see a sunflower reflected in the mirror; you will never see a frog. The reflection in the mirror is always a perfect representation of what is in front of the mirror. If the mind were a simple representation-creating device, this should also be true.

How then do we account for the fact that we make mistakes?

One way to think about how errors occur is to realize that what we see in our minds is not just a mechanical reflection of what exists outside of our minds. It is an interpretation of what is outside of our minds. Let's throw out the metaphor of a mirror and use the metaphor of a painting. A painter can look at a landscape and recreate it on a canvas using paint. The painting will not be a perfect reflection of the scene. The quality and diversity of paint colors available and the skill of the painter are just a few of the many factors that will influence the final character of the painting and create differences between it and the landscape as viewed by the naked eye.

And so it is with the images we hold in our minds. They are not perfect reflections of the world; they are interpretations of the world. Our perceptions of the world are more like paintings that we create than reflections in a mirror. We are not passive in relationship to our perception of reality; we are partially responsible for creating it.

Central to the thinking of Charles Sanders Peirce was the belief that we could never assume that any of our perceptions or ideas were completely free of wrong assumptions. Our reality is built from layers of interpretation, and any errors of interpretation that exist in one layer will be transferred to the next.

Let's go back to our metaphor of a painter. Imagine that a painter paints a landscape. The landscape on the page may be beautiful, but it will not be a perfect reflection of the landscape in front of him or her. Now let us imagine that this painting is given to another painter who tries to paint the landscape based on what he or she sees in this picture. Then that painting is given to another painter who uses it as a model for a third painting, and so on. If we could take the one thousandth painting that was painted and bring that one back to the original landscape, I wonder how different it would be.

Peirce saw our own thoughts build in a similar way to paintings that become models for other paintings. We see something and develop a thought about it. That thought becomes the object of another thought and that thought the object of another. This happens over and over and over again. Any preconceptions or errors in judgment get passed into future thoughts and on to others when we communicate ideas, so we can never assume that what we think is an accurate reflection of reality. Because no matter how hard you try to be objective you always have some error—and probably a great deal of it—built into your thinking. Our current understanding of truth sits on a mountain of ideas and assumptions that inevitably contain innumerable inconsistencies, errors, and fallacies. No idea can ever be assumed to be true in any final sense. Peirce spoke of this principle as *fallibilism*.

Our attempts to understand the universe are akin to standing on a beach for a few hours peering through a drinking straw and then drawing conclusions about the nature and history of life on Earth.

Most of us feel paralyzed at the thought of being faced with this degree of uncertainty; Peirce felt the opposite. To Peirce this degree of uncertainty was the safest assumption to make. He points out that all of our knowledge is derived through the practice of generalization. In an essay called "Fallibilism, Continuity, and Evolution" he explains that all human reasoning comes through a process of "judging the proportion of something in a whole collection by the proportion found in a sample." We observe a tiny amount of the universe, and from that sample we create general ideas about what is true everywhere else. The law of gravity, as an example, was generated from watching objects fall to the earth, and it was initially assumed to be a universal law. Only later did we realize that we had made a mistake by assuming that the behavior of objects on one planet in this vast universe was typical throughout the rest of the universe. From Peirce's point of view we are one species on one planet, and that means the knowledge we have about the universe is severely limited.

Peirce was a bold and fearless inquirer partly because he had come to peace with what he saw as the extreme limitation of human understanding. We can never be absolutely certain of anything because we are always making judgments based on what we can observe, and we can never observe every possible occurrence of any phenomenon. We experience the universe from the surface of one planet out of trillions upon trillions. We have only a few thousand years of recorded history on a planet nearly five billion years old. And the tiny slice of the universe that we are aware of is seen through the very limited filter of the perceptual and intellectual apparatus of the human form. Our attempts to understand the universe are akin to standing on a beach for a few hours peering through a drinking straw and then drawing conclusions about the nature and history of life on Earth. The sample of reality that we are able to investigate in comparison to the totality of the universe is minuscule, and so Peirce didn't presume to offer final solutions to the mysteries of existence; he wanted only to find the next best step forward for humanity to follow.

No truth should be assumed to be finally true. Truth is always in the process of building toward some final truth that we all create together. The truth as Peirce imagined it is what we are all coming to. It is what will be agreed upon in the end when every perspective and all points of view have been taken into consideration. In his review of a book called *The Works of George Berkeley*, Peirce writes:

> There is, then, to every question a true answer, a final conclusion, to which the opinion of every man is constantly gravitating. He may for a time recede from it, but give him more experience and time for consideration, and he will finally approach it. The individual may not live to reach the truth; there is a residuum of error in every individual's opinions. No matter; it remains that there is a definite opinion to which the mind of man is, on the whole and in the long run, tending.

eight

THE REALITY OF THE UNKNOWN

In a recent online *New York Times* piece, the columnist Errol Morris explains that there are things that we know; there are things that we know that we don't know; and there are things that we don't know that we don't know. This latter group is composed of "unknown unknowns."

James, like Peirce, was very concerned with the unknown. And like his friend he realized that humanity was adrift in a sea of unknown unknowns. In a lecture called "Pragmatism and Religion," James offered a metaphor to portray our true relation to the universe:

> I believe . . . that we stand in much the same relation to the whole of the universe as our canine and feline pets do to the whole of human life. They inhabit our drawing-rooms and libraries. They take part in scenes of whose significance they have no inkling. They are merely tangent to curves of history the beginnings and ends and forms of which pass

wholly beyond their ken. So we are tangents to the wider life of things.

James realized that those things that "we know that we don't know" are the limit of our imagination. I can imagine what I don't know. I don't know many scientific and cultural facts, the distance to the nearest star, the president of Montenegro, and so on. But I know there are such facts, and I readily admit to my ignorance of them.

The unknown unknowns, on the other hand, lie outside of my existing reference points. They are too far out of my box to hold in mind. Take a moment to think about it. Make a mental list of some things that you know that you don't know. Now make a mental list of some things that you don't know that you don't know. It is impossible to know where to start.

The goal of inquiry is not to come to the end of inquiry, but to continually open up new avenues for further investigation …

The early pragmatists were very respectful of the existence of truth beyond our current ability to imagine. James and Peirce both assumed that what we know about reality (and even what we can imagine about reality) is only a tiny part of the totality of what is real. In response they created a form of inquiry and philosophical attitude that was dramatically open-ended. "Never block the road to inquiry" was Peirce's motto, and what he meant was that your efforts to inquire should never lead to a point where no further inquiry is possible. The goal of inquiry is not to come to the end of inquiry, but to continually open up new avenues for further investigation, because no matter what answers we find they will never be the final truth.

James used this philosophy as the basis for outlining a way of life that allowed us to effectively live in the unknown. To function in a universe so radically full of uncertainty, the first thing that we must do is liberate our thinking, and one of the ways that our thinking gets stuck is through the process of conceptualization. "Vicious intellectualism" was the term James used to describe how our concepts about reality can hinder the process of inquiry if in our minds they stand in place of what is actually real. Human beings create concepts. When we recognize something to be real or true, we label it with a word or an idea. Once a concept is created we tend to believe in the truth of that concept and simultaneously see things that contradict it as false. If I see something and believe that it is a cat, I believe at the same time that it is not a dog, a mouse, or a fire truck. In my mind the positive assertion of something being a cat includes the negative assertion of it not being a dog, a mouse, or a fire truck. What if we are talking about the concept of God? If we label one idea as "God," then we are simultaneously labeling every other definition for this word as "not God." James realized that when talking about more subtle and significant concepts the habit of vicious intellectualism causes big trouble—as in, "My definition of God is true, and therefore yours can only be false."

James' conception of vicious intellectualism can be understood as the assumption that the way we see things is the way they actually are. What James meant by vicious intellectualism is similar to what Wilfrid Sellars meant by the myth of the given. The reason he was so concerned about it was because he saw how our ability to inquire is profoundly impaired by the negative assumptions that get smuggled into our thinking. We never think to question these negative assumptions because they are hidden from view inside our concepts. And if we fail to question our concepts we tend to follow paths of inquiry that can only proceed by expanding on what is already known. In James' opinion we hold too tightly to the truth in hand. We are only willing to inquire at the borders of what we already know, avoiding the vast oceans of the unknown that surround us.

The philosophy of pragmatism was meant to offer a different approach to inquiry. In pragmatic inquiry, truth is not seen as a collection of knowable facts, but rather an ongoing process of investigation. No truth should be considered final; rather all truth is the jumping off point to further investigation because whatever we think is true today will inevitably yield to bigger and more encompassing conceptions of truth tomorrow. For James that meant developing the willingness to inquire directly into what we don't already know by focusing on the anomalies and oddities that don't fit into our current understanding.

James wanted to focus more attention on the outer fringes of what we know. The next big idea doesn't come from the center—it comes from the dim outer edge, where the light of what we know fades into the blackness of the unknown unknowns beyond. James risked his career and his reputation as an academic and a scientist to study things that others thought were absurdities. As president of the Society for Psychical Research, he studied spirits, mediums, and life after death. Most scientists felt that studying these strange, unexplainable occurrences was a waste of time because they strayed too far from what we already knew to be true. James, on the other hand, felt that they were the first place we should look because they already proved that what we know isn't enough.

nine

EVOLUTIONARY EXISTENTIALISM

Peirce and James were lifelong friends and colleagues carrying out distinctly different philosophical agendas. Peirce's philosophical aspiration was to lay down the foundation for a philosophical system that could explain the existence and evolution of everything. He complained later in his life that James had taken the philosophy of pragmatism and anchored it too narrowly to merely human concerns. James was concerned with explaining our human experience of life and developing a philosophy that would allow us to act with confidence in the face of insecurity.

To understand James it is important to recognize that his concerns were existential. The characteristic that most unifies existentialists is their belief that human beings must look squarely into the ultimate mysterious emptiness that lies at the core of reality. In the face of this overwhelming uncertainty we must not cower or turn our heads toward the past. Truth is not something you search for. It is not a hidden treasure to find. Truth to an existentialist is something you stand for—a stake that each of us must plant firmly in the face of doubt. The future is not waiting to be discovered; it is what we will build through the stands that we take.

In his book *Irrational Man*, William Barrett comments that "of all non-European philosophers William James probably best deserves to be labeled an Existentialist." Barrett goes on to assert that it would be more accurate to call James an existentialist than a pragmatist. Indeed, many of the themes and concerns that occupy James' philosophy are those that preoccupied the European existentialists, not the least of which was his defense of faith. James took on a powerful scientific world and risked his own reputation by defending the right to believe even without direct evidence. James' essay "The Will to Believe" was his manifesto on faith.

In his defense of faith James was challenging a philosophical position known as *logical positivism*. You and I and almost anyone likely to read this book is probably at heart a logical positivist without even knowing it. In fact, for most of us anything else is hard to relate to. Logical positivism dictates that something is only true if there is conclusive evidence that demonstrates it to be true. In other words, truth has to be proven before it is accepted. Nothing should be accepted on faith.

James questioned this view. Is it possible to wait for conclusive evidence before we believe in something? Why do we think that conclusive evidence is the best way to know what is true? James believed that ultimately truth had to be a matter of faith. Even the position of logical positivism was a matter of faith in the end because the idea that waiting for conclusive evidence is the best way to validate truth is itself taken on faith.

The idea that waiting for conclusive evidence is the best way to validate truth is itself taken on faith.

There is so much that we see as reality that is actually nothing more than unquestioned beliefs that we have unconsciously accepted on faith. James realized that these deep beliefs often don't result from evidence. Consciously or unconsciously we are choosing to believe in these ideas and then acting as if they were true. We are, in effect, staking our lives on them. These assumptions might have been handed to us by our culture; they might have been dictated by religion; or they might have come from experiences in our own life—most likely a combination of all three. Rest assured, however, somewhere underneath everything there are many presumptions about reality that you accept as true without conclusive evidence and perhaps without even realizing it. We are, in the end, acting on faith.

As James saw it, whatever we choose to believe in, or choose not to believe in, will affect the way we act and live, so how we exercise our "will to believe" is of the utmost importance. We stand on our beliefs, and from there we push off into an uncertain future where the results of our actions will either strengthen our confidence in our beliefs or force us to reconsider them. Rather than holding back and waiting for proof, James prefers to lean forward into life, accepting the reality that many of our decisions must be made on faith, doing his best to consciously choose what to believe, and then acting wholeheartedly as if the truth of those beliefs were assured. The process of human life is then a relentless affair of jumping consciously yet somewhat blindly into the future and then continually adjusting and readjusting our beliefs based on the results.

In his essay "Great Men and Their Environment," James directly examines the evolutionary significance of our choices. As he sees it the people we become can act as guideposts that lead the evolution of culture forward. He opens the essay with the question, "What are the causes that make communities change from generation to generation?" And he concludes that, "The difference is due to the accumulated influences of individuals, of their examples, their initiatives, and their decisions." James' brand of evolutionary existentialism rests on the conscious exercise of our will to believe. By choosing which ideas to believe in and then acting on them, we embody new possibilities for human existence. Once embodied these possibilities either compel others to adopt them or are rejected and disappear. The evolution of society occurs as embodied ideas enter into a process of cultural selection. Great individuals embody or, as Emerson would have said, "represent" possibilities that the rest of humanity follow until they become cultural norms. We can take an increasingly active part in this process by becoming more consciously aware of the beliefs that we are choosing to believe in and embody.

HUMAN LIFE IS A RISK

Human life is a risk.
To believe in anything is a risk.
To not believe is also a risk.

Anything we do is a risk.
Not doing anything is also a risk.

We might decide to avoid all risk by believing
nothing and doing nothing.
That is very risky.

Better to believe and act wholeheartedly,
always ready to think again and
change our minds

THE CIRCUMSTANCES AROUND US ARE CHANGING FASTER THAN WE CAN.

The world and everything in it is changing all the time, and our beliefs about it all must change at least as quickly.

Often they don't.

We find ourselves stuck in beliefs whose time has passed, not knowing which questions to ask or what direction to take forward.

These concluding essays outline the evolutionary challenge of our time and the role that philosophical inquiry can play in meeting that challenge.

ten

OUR EVOLUTIONARY CRISIS

What is a crisis? I would propose that a crisis occurs when our circumstances change more rapidly than we can change in response. When we find ourselves in crisis, we are overwhelmed by circumstances that are changing faster than we can, and we are called upon to find an extraordinary means of response.

The awareness of a crisis tends to bring with it a sense of panic and an associated desperation for immediate action. Under such circumstances we are tempted to disregard philosophical considerations even though they are often at the heart of the original reasons for the crisis. The twentieth-century anthropologist and philosopher Gregory Bateson has provocatively stated that,

> The major problems in the world are the result of the difference between the way nature works and the way man thinks.

We base our actions on our understanding of the nature of reality and the way the world works. That understanding is partly made up of our consciously held beliefs about what is true, but much more so by unconsciously held convictions about what is true. To the extent that our convictions about what is true are inaccurate we will find ourselves unable to respond appropriately to our challenges and problems. And it is the work of philosophical introspection that allows us to bring awareness to our unconscious assumptions so that they may be examined, altered, or discarded completely.

Many of our world's greatest challenges are symptoms of an overarching evolutionary crisis. This overarching crisis is caused by the fact that the circumstances of our world are changing at a faster and faster pace, and human beings are not able to keep up. Our problems seem to be compounding because we are not able to respond adequately to one crisis before the next arises, and then there is another and another. We sometimes feel like we are being buried under a pile of insurmountable problems.

No one solution to any given problem is going to remedy this situation. What needs to change is our ability to respond—our response-ability. Human beings need to learn how to respond faster. We have to learn to uncover unconscious assumptions, examine them, and then change the way we act with greater and greater speed and efficiency. We must all become high-speed, super-efficient philosophers and accelerating agents of change. In times of crisis, especially evolutionary crisis, philosophy is far from a luxury.

To increase the rate at which we change, we need to examine our relationship to the feeling of change. Isn't it true that we have all been conditioned to experience trepidation—ranging from anxiety to terror—whenever we encounter a new situation or circumstance? We have been conditioned to be cautious of anything new, which leads us to avoid change. In order for us to be able to keep up with our world's accelerating rate of change, one of the first things that we need to change is the way we feel about change.

What needs to change is our ability to respond—our response-ability.

For thousands of years human beings believed that the universe was fundamentally unchanging. It was a static stage upon which the drama of life played out. In such a universe "change" feels "bad." If things are supposed to remain fixed, then any time we feel things changing we instinctively feel fear and insecurity—something is wrong. Isn't that what happens? When things start to change, don't you get uneasy, don't your alarm bells start to ring? We are conditioned to fear change.

Now that we realize we live in an evolutionary universe and that we as a human family need to evolve, we must learn to feel uneasy when things don't change. Imagine traveling in a train. If it comes to a halt in the middle of the tracks, you get uneasy and imagine that something is wrong because the train is supposed to move. An evolutionary universe is also supposed to move. We need to develop a more positive sensibility toward experiences of change so that we won't automatically recoil from change and miss important opportunities for growth as a result.

eleven

PHILOSOPHY IS NOT A LUXURY

The premise of this book is that philosophy is not a luxury item that we can afford to do away with. It is a necessity for a well-lived human life—especially when we are challenged, or worse, when we find ourselves in times of crisis.

When we face mounting challenges and overwhelming crises, we are tempted to see philosophy as a luxury item that we can no longer afford. It's not! In fact, in the face of overwhelming difficulties, philosophy, which is the pursuit of truth, becomes more important, not less.

Why? Because what we believe is true dictates how we act, and how we act creates the world we live in.

If you recognize some part of yourself that protests this statement, look at it. It might be insisting that, "My actions are not dictated to me. I do what I want to do. I am a free, independent person."

Most of us believe that nothing can dictate our actions to us—not even our own beliefs. What if it isn't true? What if you were to discover that you could only ever act in accordance with what you believed to be true—that you were a prisoner to your own beliefs and always would be? How would you relate to philosophy and to your quest to examine what is true then?

I would not go so far as to say that there is no free will. I appreciate James' insight that our freedom is not found in our ability to self-direct our actions, but rather in our ability to choose what we believe. James also recognized that the world we create as a society depends on the truths we share. His words from the essay "The Will to Believe" still have something powerful to say to us today:

> A social organism of any sort whatever, large or small, is what it is because each member proceeds to his own duty with a trust that the other members will simultaneously do theirs. Wherever a desired result is achieved by the cooperation of many independent persons, its existence as a fact is a pure consequence of the precursive faith in one another of those immediately concerned. A government, an army, a commercial system, a ship, a college, an athletic team, all exist on this condition, without which not only is nothing achieved, but nothing is even attempted.

If we agree that the world is created by the results of our individual and collective actions, and we know that the world needs to change, then we have to discover a new truth—together. Philosophy, as the pursuit of truth, is critical and must become a collective endeavor so that we can change the world by changing the way we think about the world.

Times of crisis are definitely times when we need to focus our attention and our energy. Some things that were important become luxuries that we can no longer afford. Philosophy is not one of these. In times of crisis, more than ever we must examine what we believe to be true and why we believe it, so we can discover higher, deeper, and more encompassing truths that will lead to actions that will change the world for the better.

WHAT BELIEFS ARE YOU HOLDING ONTO RIGHT NOW?

What beliefs are you holding onto right now?

How are you evaluating the validity of those beliefs?

Are you ready to let them go when it is time to change?

ABOUT JEFF CARREIRA

Jeff Carreira originally received an undergraduate degree in physics and spent five years working as a research engineer before realizing that life's deepest questions could not be answered through science alone. He decided to work in a more humanitarian field and received a master's degree in education and spent seven years working as a special education teacher and school administrator.

He is currently the director of education at the educational nonprofit called EnlightenNext. In that position he creates and organizes a global network of spiritual and philosophical education programs and has trained over one hundred other individuals to teach worldwide. He also co-leads The Evolutionary Collective where he supports and facilitates the development of individuals through an intensive yearlong program of engagement. Carreira believes that human beings at the start of the twenty-first century must build a strong sense of global connectedness rooted in profound philosophical and spiritual values so that we can evolve to higher possibilities of relatedness and cooperation.

He is passionate about philosophy because he is passionate about the power that ideas have to shape the way we see ourselves and the way we live. He is available to speak to audiences that are interested in the power of ideas. Jeff's enthusiasm for learning is infectious, and he is particularly interested in addressing student groups and inspiring them to develop their